The Temple Gate Called Beautiful

Selected books by David Kirby

The House on Boulevard St.: New and Selected Poems

Ultra-Talk: Johnny Cash, the Mafia, Shakespeare, Drum Music, St. Teresa of Avila, and 17 Other Colossal Topics of Conversation

I Think I Am Going to Call My Wife Paraguay

The Ha-Ha

What Is a Book?

The Travelling Library

The House of Blue Light

My Twentieth Century

Big-Leg Music

Saving the Young Men of Vienna

Sarah Bernhardt's Leg

The Temple Gate Called Beautiful

David Kirby

Alice James Books
Farmington, Maine

10 9 8 7 6 5 4 3 2 1

Alice James Books are published by Alice James Poetry Cooperative, Inc., an affiliate of the
University of Maine at Farmington.

ALICE JAMES BOOKS
238 MAIN STREET
FARMINGTON, ME 04938

www.alicejamesbooks.org

Library of Congress Cataloging-in-Publication Data
Kirby, David
The temple gate called beautiful / David Kirby.
    p.   cm.
ISBN-13: 978-1-882295-67-8
ISBN-10: 1-882295-67-6
I. Title.
PS3561.I66T46 2008
811'.54—dc22   2007044643

Alice James Books gratefully acknowledges support from the University of Maine at
Farmington and the National Endowment for the Arts. ❧

Permission to reprint "Encounter" from The Collected Poems, 1931-1987 by Czeslaw
Milosz is gratefully acknowledged. Copyright ©by Czeslaw Milosz Royalties, Inc.
Reprinted by permission of HarperCollins Publishers.

Cover Art: Luca Signorelli (1441-1523), detail from "Resurrection of the Dead" Fresco.
Location: Duomo, Orvieto, Italy
Photo Credit : Scala / Art Resource, NY

ACKNOWLEDGMENTS

Many thanks to the following journals where these poems (sometimes in earlier versions) first appeared:

Five Points: "The Knowledge," "The Mysteries," "The Secret Room"
Gettysburg Review: "The Measurator"
Gulf Stream: "All Earthly Hues"
Hunger Mountain: "Elvis, Be My Psychopomp"
Meridian: "Sex and Candy"
North Dakota Quarterly: "Doughboy's Bitch"
Ploughshares: "Hello, I Must Be Going"
Poetry: "Dogs Who Are Poets and Movie Stars"
Pool: "Merry Hell"
Nightsun: "Mopery With Intent To Creep"
Shade: "Letter Home on My Birthday, November 29, 2002," "Terrible Swift Sword"
Smartish Pace: "Die Meistersinger," "The Only Good Question," "The Temple Gate Called Beautiful"

CONTENTS

◆

◆

◆

◆

"God damn it," the old man said in a slow monotonous certain tone as if he were saying it to the beating of his heart. "God damn every goddamn thing to hell."

—Flannery O'Connor,

"A Late Encounter With the Enemy"

Elvis, Be My Psychopomp

Sometimes I see my dead parents: at the end of the street,
say, or just ahead of me in the ticket line. At times
they are turning into another aisle at the supermarket,
and I want to run after them as I did when I was a little boy,
and at other times, they are walking toward me and smile
when they see who it is, though when I reach to embrace them,

they vanish, like the gods in *The Iliad*.
They're my age now—or not my age, for if they are sixty,
then I am twenty again, so young and so unhappy,
though I don't know it. When Odysseus goes
to the underworld, he sees his mother, who can't speak until he sacrifices
a ram and an ewe, and she drinks their blood, though

when she does and they talk to one another, he tries
to embrace her but can't. Aeneas, too, goes to the underworld
to seek his father, Anchises—if they can, why not I?
I'd need a psychopomp, a Hermes or the Sibyl of Cumae,
and while I wish it could be "bright-eyed" Athena,
who leads Telemachus here and there in search of his father,

as I am white, male, Southern, and have lived
most of my life in the last half of the 20th century,
I think it will be Elvis who leads me through *the darkness*
of the night with shadows all about us,
as great Homer said, *through the empty halls and the desolate kingdom,*
as though walking in a wood by the light of the fitful moon

when Jupiter has hung the sky in shadow and black night
has robbed all things of their color. And when the Angel
of the Apocalypse taps on the Bible and says, "There shall be time

no longer," Elvis will say, "You get some kind
of decoder ring with that thing, man?" and I'll thank him:
        "Thank you, Elvis!" I'll cry, and he'll say, "Look, ace, I always

        played heroes in the movies, but when the director
    said 'Cut!' it was time for drugs and stupidity
and the coveting of women. The way I see it, this is my chance."
        We pass signs saying "Warning: Bridge Out"
and "Hitchhikers May Be Escaping Inmates" and before I know it,
    we're in the Valley of the Perversely Proud and Presumptuous

        and out again, and when we cross the Nail-Studded Bridge
    and I weep and say I can't walk because my feet are bleeding,
Elvis says, "Remember how, in your life, your feet were ready
        to carry you to those places where you could sin?"
When we see Lord Satan devouring sinners and excreting them
    out his backside, Elvis will say, "Let's slide on by—

        if he catches us, not only will we be dead sons of bitches,
    but so will our souls. We'll just be a bag of slop."
And we do, but not before the King of Cruelty
        sees us and cries, "Elvis! What's it like in Tupelo?"
and Elvis says, "Uh, rough! But a nurse to good lads."
    Then he mutters under his breath, and I think it's something

        about an "undead sack of shit." So far, I figure, so good.
    The trick, of course, is not getting into Hell;
it's getting out again. Bread, meat, beer, chips, ice, bait,
        smokeless tobacco, beef jerky, water for washing—
everything must be refused if you wish to leave
    the Kingdom of the Dead. We pass Hades,

        the master of Tartarus, sometimes called Plouton
    or Wealthy One because of his vast holdings:
precious metals, objects buried with the dead, the wealth

of crops that spring from his soil. And Buddy Holly
and Jimi Hendrix, and Elvis says to Jimi, "Hey,
        your dad misses you, man" and Jimi says, "Give him this"

        and tries to hand Elvis a black guitar that slithers
        and undulates as fiery streaks rise to its surface like lava
and fall back again, but Elvis knows better.
        We see Janis Joplin surrounded by devilkins
stamping their crooked legs and punching each other and snickering,
        and Elvis says, "Eating out your hand like always, mama!"

        and Janis says, "Are you shitting me?
        I'd rather be a crack whore on Melrose than Lady Paramount
of these twerps." And so we pass into The Place
        of The Bad But Not Very Bad and from there
to The Place Of The Good But Not Very Good
        and on to the Land of Joy, the resplendent glades, the happy

        wood, the meadow of the blessed where there
        is dancing and singing and wrestling and running,
and eventually we come to a little park, and there are my mom
        and dad at a table, watching the games and eating
and drinking what they ate and drank in life: fried chicken, martinis,
        lemon meringue pie, and I'm thinking, Martinis?

        and Elvis reads my mind and says, "Beats the hell
        out of ram's blood, huh, buddy?" My father is silent,
as he always was, but my mother begins to chatter away:
        "You're Elvis Presley, aren't you? You've got
a lot to answer for, young man. What's with the hips
        and the hound dog and that stuff in your hair?"

        And Elvis says, "You think those days were something,
        lady, you ought to see what's going on up there now."
And I try to talk to her, but she can't hear me, so I tell Elvis,

"Ask her why she died. Say 'What is death, anyway?'"
And he does, and she says, "When I was alone
and my new life began, it wasn't to my liking.

I missed my husband so much, his wit,
his merry ways, and life was sweet no longer, so I died."
Which is a pretty speech, but I don't remember my father
as merry or witty, and he doesn't, either,
because when I look over at him, he shrugs and smiles shyly,
as if to say, If she wants to remember it that way, let her.

The other dead draw closer, and Elvis licks his lips:
"We can't stay," he says, and I cry, "Goodbye, Mommy!"
but she's eating her pie again, though my dad raises his hand
just perceptibly and sticks out his thumb
and little finger and makes the *shaka* and wiggles it, the way
surfers do in Hawai'i. We pass through the Gate of Horn

and make our way back, and just as I can see
the fires of my native land, Elvis says, "See ya," and I say,
"See ya, Elvis!" and then, "Elvis, wait!"
Because the challenge for mythic heroes
is not slaying the enemy or freeing the oppressed, it's telling
the story to those who have never seen a dragon.

But Elvis says, "Aw, just listen to the songs, man,"
and I say, "But they're not in order. Also—I'm sorry—
some of them are bad!" He shrugs and says,
"That's the only way to tell the story" and disappears,
and I'm wondering what he means by that.
I wonder if I'll ever see my dead parents again,

and if I do—at the end of the street, say,
as Barbara and I take our morning walk, and I look up,
and, suddenly, there they are—if my father will look

at me and smile and look down, the way he did in life,
as my mother floats by, regal as always, oblivious, almost,
    and I say, "Mommy! Remember? I just saw you

    in the other world! You were drinking martinis!
    Don't be dead!" And Barbara says,
"Who are you talking to?" and they go right by,
    and just as they're about to walk away, maybe forever
this time, my mother rolls her hips, ever so gently,
    and my dad says, "All right, now, mamma—shake that thing!"

Merry Hell

When I think of the books and authors we used
to joke about as kids, of *The Tiger's Revenge*
   by Claude Balls, say, or I. C. Manybutts' *Under
the Bleachers,* I ask myself: Okay, say a woman
         is named Smith or Brown and she marries a man
named Manybutts and does the old-fashioned thing
   and changes her name to his, still, what kind of

mother would then name her child Isadora
Charlene? Manybutts: it sounds like a creature in a Bosch painting,
   doesn't it? Like someone or something that
would be perfectly at home in a landscape
         swarming with birds wearing soup strainers
on their heads, couples copulating in floating crystals
   that bob and curtsy on a wine-red river, a monk

hurtling through the air as flames burst from his ass.
Like you, whenever someone says "Manybutts" to me,
   I think of Lucian of Samosata, in whose *Dialogues
of the Dead* Charon upbraids Menippus for trying to cross
         the Styx without paying, though
Menippus says he baled, he rowed, he was the only passenger
   who didn't weep, and that if someone has to pay,

it should be Hermes, who brought him there
in the first place, though when Hermes refuses,
   Charon blames him for bringing this dog
of a Menippus who chattered during the whole
         boat ride and mocked and jeered at the other
passengers and sang as they lamented.
   Is this not what the ancients call Merry Hell,

the place where you or Menippus or Alfred
E. Newman skate blithely over the sufferings of others?
    The celebrated English actress
Mrs. Patrick Campbell said that success is going from
        failure to failure without losing
your enthusiasm, but I wonder how enthusiastic
    Mrs. Patrick Campbell would be about going

    from, say, the Mountain of Unbelievers
and Heretics, where the wicked
    are tossed from heat to ice and back again,
to the Valley of Fires for Those Who
        Commit Evil Upon Evil, where the Prince
of Hell casts damned souls into fiery torments as he exhales
    and then breathes them in again. Or, worse,

    if Ereshkigal unleashed the "sixty miseries"
against her as she does to her own sister Ishtar
    in *Gilgamesh*: "Go, Namtar, lock her up in my palace,"
shrieks Ereshkigal, "and release against her
        the sixty miseries: misery of the eyes against
her eyes, misery of the sides against her sides,
    misery of the heart against her heart, misery

    of the feet against her feet, of the head against
her head—against every part of her,
    against her whole body!" Yet Hell is big,
for its architects are giants: Homer, Virgil, Plato, Augustine,
        Dante, Bosch, Michelangelo,
Milton, Goethe, and Blake, not to mention Satan
    and, of course, God. Hell has many mansions,

    some funny, some not so, and room abundant
for hookah-puffing caterpillars, dogs dressed
    in high heels and ball gowns, devils kicking

sinners into nets as though they are soccer balls.
    In Merry Hell, everything's okay. Problems
tend to solve themselves in Merry Hell,
    and fuel bills are low in winter. If you merely

    gave your child a bad start in life, you'd probably
go to Hell, but not the worst part. It's hard
    to get published, and I. C. Manybutts is a successful
author now, and who's to say that's not because
    of the wondrous name her mother gave her,
as did the moms of Phil R. Upp, gas station
    attendant, or all those dentists named Payne.

Doughboy's Bitch

I'm listening to two students talking, and one is saying
    there was a guy in high school who looked just like
the Pillsbury Doughboy, so they called him "Doughboy" and
    poked him when he walked by, and the other student says,
        "What if you went to jail and Doughboy were the king
of the jail? What if you were Doughboy's bitch?"

and I can see the first guy is really thinking about this,
    how some serious payback might be
waiting for him out there, his whole life flying through the air
    like a game of Monopoly you play for three days
        and then, just when everybody has bought all their hotels
and railroads and has their little markers in place

and their play-money bills neatly tucked away in tidy stacks,
    some guy, some asshole of which every family has
at least one, sticks his finger under the edge of the board
    and flip! You're Doughboy's bitch, a word I hate, though
        in this context it means, not "generic female," but "seriously
out-of-luck male prisoner subject to rough sex,

involuntary laundry duty, and other coercion at the hands of
    of his cellmate-oppressor." I didn't even think
of the nuns at St. Agnes as bitches when they caught me raking
    my lima beans into a planter at age six and told me
        it was a mortal sin, though I do remember thinking,
Wait, I'm going to be in Hell with Judas?

I didn't think of the nuns as anything, though I knew
    I had more control over my life than the holy sisters
were letting on, even if earlier that year my little beagle

Candy had begun to drool and wheeze and have seizures,
     and I'd got out my chemistry set
to try and come up with a cure, but I couldn't, and Candy died.

Later, when I was living in Baltimore and had to get
     to Annapolis fast because my girlfriend was breaking up
with me, I got in line at the Greyhound station behind
     twenty other guys, probably half of them in a similar fix,
          and waited and waited and finally walked across the street
to a pay phone and called and, through the window,

saw the agent pick up the phone and reserve my ticket
     while the guys in line shook their heads in disgust.
I was Doughboy that day, at least till I got to Annapolis.
     My two students are talking about something else now,
          but I'm guessing that the first one
is thinking about his future, thinking it's a dog-eat-dog world,

that sometimes you eat the dog, sometimes the dog eats you.
     Stuntmen say if you see the stunt's
going bad, don't act scared, because if you do, the shot will be ruined,
     and you will have died for nothing. But how often
          does that happen? Most days,
you're lucky. Most days, you're the teenaged George Harrison,

afraid to go to Germany and from there to stardom
     because he is afraid of German food,
afraid it won't be what he's used to, and then learning
     they have "ham sarnies" there, too, just ham,
          bread, and butter, like the ones you get in Liverpool,
with nothing funny on them, nothing you can't pronounce.

For the rest of the class, my normally-chatty student
     is silent, and, yeah, sure, almost certainly he's thinking
about the childhood he's got to leave one of these days

and the adult world he's stepping into, like it or not.
    That night Barbara and I are eating at Chez Pierre,
and I'm talking with Karen, the owner, and I say, "Karen,

do you remember that night a few months back when you shook
    your finger in Mr. Turner's face and shouted,
'You're not welcome in my restaurant any more, Mr. Turner!'
    because he got abusive when he couldn't be seated
        near the 'colored girl' who was singing that evening,
and then that food fight broke out, the three drunks

throwing *daube de boeuf* at each other, the ceiling,
    the other patrons, one of whom, according to the rumors
that began to fly through the restaurant, was lying
    unconscious, and then dead, on the women's room floor,
        neither of which turned out to be true?"
And Karen says, "David, I'd forgotten all about that night!"

The next time I see my student, I'll want to say, Forget Doughboy,
    or he'll turn you into your own bitch.
Forget everyone: the faithless, the unjust, the dead. . . .
    In Book IX of *The Odyssey*, Odysseus and his men have
        a terrible day, and several die, and finally the survivors put
into shore, set up camp, make fires, and only then do they weep.

Dogs Who Are Poets and Movie Stars

As I walk up Sixth Avenue, I pass a dog being dragged
down Eighth Street by its impatient owner,
        and the dog is looking over its shoulder belligerently
at something on the other side of Sixth, so I, too, look
        when I reach the intersection, and I expect to see another dog,

of course, but there's no one there except a woman
with big boobs, so I ask myself, Is the dog really a man who's
        been turned into a dog for staring too often and too long
at comely women? The ancient Greeks made rather a specialty
        of this sort of thing, didn't they, of seeing to it that chaps

who didn't behave themselves went through some sort
of metamorphic comeuppance? Do not the wolves
        and lions on Circe's island frighten Odysseus's men
by jumping up on them and wagging their tails
        because they are rogues turned into animals

by the enchantress? I bet the Eighth Street dog
had been a movie star, because everything I read
        about movie stars suggests they can't control themselves
for more than five minutes. Julianne Moore lives
        on Eleventh, and John, who lives on Twelfth,

says that if I will take his Cairn Terrier Henry
for a walk and we run into Ms. Moore, I can talk to her:
        she won't stop for me, but she'll stop to talk to Henry,
and then I can talk to her. But whether or not I run into
        Ms. Moore, I would certainly have to clean up after Henry

when he does his business in order to be in compliance
with city sanitation code, and I'd rather miss out on
        a conversation with Ms. Moore than clean up after Henry.

Whenever I think of Julianne Moore, I want to call her
    Marianne Moore, of whom I've thought many times

    more than I have of Julianne. Would I run the risk
of having to clean up after Henry to meet Marianne Moore?
        Almost certainly, since she's dead, ha, ha! Sometimes
I read the dog biographies from the pet adoption page of the paper
    and think how pleasant it would be to own Shadow,

    say, a "3½ year-old neutered purebred, Llewellin setter,
housebroken," though I'd probably re-name him
        Llewellin. Or maybe Rebel, a "3 year-old male,
short black and tan coat, good with cats and children," but not Josie,
    a "2½ year-old spayed purebred basset hound, no cats

    or small children"! My mother's name was Josie.
But a dog who doesn't like cats or children is not a dog
        you'd want to own, even though taking a nip out
of Tabby's hindquarters or Josh or Kimberly's chubby
    little leg is very much *au naturel* for your dog, very much

    the very essence of dogginess, you might say. Not that
there aren't good dogs out there: Harry and George,
        for example, two therapy dogs who work in
the school system, good boys who put their heads
    on their paws and listen to stories read by children

    who don't read well, who are mocked by other kids
when they get a word wrong or turn their Rs into Ws,
        yet Harry and George say nothing when the kids say
"how" instead of "who" or stutter or stumble over a word
    they've never seen before. I'm going to treat each dog

    as though he or she is a dead celebrity, is Errol Flynn
or Carole Lombard or W. H. Auden or Marilyn Monroe,
        a dead actor or poet. I myself think it would be

excellent to be a celebrity some day, and if I am one,
    then I should expect to be a dog later. And then

    perhaps a celebrity again: who knows when this sort
of thing is going to run its course? Circe drugs
    Odysseus's men and turns them into pigs
with *pigs' heads and grunts and bristles, pigs all over*
    except that their minds were the same as before,

    yet when they are changed back, they are *younger*
than they were before, and handsomer and taller.
    On the corner of Bleecker Street I do see a celebrity,
and one that it is a very great pleasure to see, too,
    so far out of his element; it is Gérard Dépardieu.

Terrible Swift Sword

Finally I get my nerve up to take the #19 bus
all the way to the end of the line to visit Finsbury Park Mosque,
    site of the one-year anniversary "celebration"
        of the September 11 attacks and the place
where radical Islamists from all over Europe come to plot
    the downfall of the West, and it's a typical
        sun-sets-at-four London day, and just as I'm thinking,

How will I know where to get off?, the bus jogs onto
St. Thomas Road and there it is, dome on the right, minaret on the left,
    both topped by these terrible swords—
        no, quarter moons, but still terrible-looking, all pointy
and sinister, moons falling to earth to sever and maim,
    not fun moons like the ones in Shakespeare
        or "That's Amore." And there's a guy outside resting

his arms on the railing, but one of his arms is not only
just a stump but a badly-stitched one, as though it had been
    dressed in the field or, worse, a basement after an accident
        in a bomb lab, and I think, Shit, I can't do this, but then
maybe it happened the usual way, i.e., not in war against
    the Great Satan that is me and Barbara and the boys
        and a bunch of other harmless individuals but, you know . . .

hunting accident. Job-site mishap. Domestic argument
that went a little too far, that sort of thing. Besides,
    just over his shoulder, I can see a card rack. Christmas cards!
        No, not Christmas cards, but there's definitely a gift shop,
meaning stuff for sale, meaning my money's as good
    as anyone else's, so I get up my moxie and enter,
        and there's every radical Islamic doodad you'd ever want:

Bin Laden tapes and books and posters, a perfume called
"Secret Man," slippers, caps, and three sizes of toenail clippers—
    child, adult, and veterinary strength—
        as well as books such as Moulana Majazazami's
Guidance for a Muslim Wife, which contains advice like
        "When a husband calls his wife at night to have relations
    with her and she refuses without a valid Shari reason,

        she is cursed throughout the night by the angels,"
and a copy of which I buy for Barbara.
    There's also a box for clothes to be donated
        to the children of Kashmir, which gives me an opening
to talk to the great fat man behind the gift-shop counter
        who even gives me a couple of plastic bags
        to put the clothes in, but I figure I'm about as likely

        to do that as I am to buy those nail clippers
and the "Secret Man" perfume, because (a) Do I want
    to mark myself as a sightseer or, worse, a snoop
        and occasion the reappearance of the guy with
the missing arm and, besides, (b) Do I really want
        to make a contribution, however small, to the funding
        of terrorists?, the answer to both these questions being "no,"

        which is also the answer to my third and final question,
which is (c) Do I want to turn on CNN some morning
    and see a guy in a Yemeni courtroom wearing one
        of my Gap shirts? But I have to buy the book, which I do,
and then it's back to central London and my second mission
        of the day, which is to find a gym for my colleagues
        Joe Donoghue and Sissi Carroll, who will be teaching here

        during the spring term, and I've seen ads—
adverts—for Esporta Health Club, which is near
    where Joe and Sissi will be living, so I "pop 'round,"
        as the English say, and the two Esporta staffers

couldn't be snarkier, couldn't be more disdainful
         or willfully obtuse. No, they don't have a brochure.
    No, they can't see why I'm enquiring on behalf

         of someone other than myself. No, I'll have
to purchase a temporary membership before proceeding.
    No, they can neither explain their fees nor understand
         why I'd want an explanation. Finally,
I observe that what I'm proposing appears to be just a little
         too difficult for them and ask if I might possibly
    speak to a supervisor, but, no, they're afraid

         that's not possible, either, so it's back out into
the London cold for me and hard cheese for Joe and Sissi,
    though I'm sure they'll find a health club somewhere,
         and I'm halfway home when I realize, Fuck!
The one-armed guy and the great fat man
         at Finsbury Park Mosque were nicer to me than
    the two toffee-nosed narcissists at Esporta Health Club!

         Fuck! Ever want to pull your clothes off
and just start screaming? Sure, you'd be arrested, but at least
    things would make sense for a couple of minutes.
         I feel as though steam's about to start leaking out
the side of my neck when I notice that the marquee
         in front of Metropolitan Community Church advertises
    a noon meditation, so I stop in and ask the nice lady

         if the meditation is non-sectarian, and she says yes,
it's like yoga, only "without the plinky-plonky music."
    So I pretzel up my legs and begin to follow
         the nice lady's gentle directives, and, sure enough,
it doesn't take long for my fury to not only abate
         but turn into something like calm, even serenity, say,
    though from time to time there are fits of coughing

like mortar fire, and when I open one eye,
I notice most of my fellow devotees look as though
    they spent the night on a steam grate and are probably here
    more for the free doughnuts than the spirituality,
but I hang in there, and, sure enough,
    my black-and-white world view begins to break up
    into a scattering of lovely grays as I recall the story

    Willie Nelson tells about a guy named
Ben Dorsey who used to work for Johnny Cash,
    and he had a bunch of suits that Johnny had given him,
    and one day Ben was walking down the street
in front of the Grand Ole Opry, and this guy
    comes up with a guitar in his hand and thinks Ben
    is one of the stars because of the fancy suit,

    so the guy says, "How do you get started
in this business?" and Ben says, "Ain't but
    one way, hoss. You start at the bottom,
    you go right to the top. Don't mess
with that in-between shit." And, sure, it'd be nice
    if things worked that way, as it does in most movies,
    though not in life—maybe you've noticed.

    Ah, London: I've lived in you four months,
and I still don't know which way to look
    when I cross your streets. One night
    I see Harold Pinter in a pub, and the next day
I read that producer Sam Spiegel once told Pinter
    "The secret of happiness is whores."
    Maybe. Probably not for the whores, though.

    During the Monica Lewinsky scandal,
my mother-in-law visits us in France,
    and when I say the French aren't as upset
        about it as a lot of Americans seem to be,

she says, "Yeah, well, it's a way of life for them, isn't it?"
    though I can't tell whether she means lying,
  oral sex, lying about oral sex, or all three.

    When the meditation session is over,
the nice lady offers us a cup of tea,
  and a man wearing three overcoats motions me
      into a corner and says, "May I tell you
a joke for a tiny piece of change?" I'm so happy
    I could kiss him. They're okay by me, the English,
    even if we don't speak the same language.

The Only Good Question

"And then your looks leave," she says,
and I can see them heading out the swinging door:
    your taut skin, your high fanny, your shiny eyes and hair,
and I ask myself, Where do they go,
       your looks, which sounds like a good question,
    and certainly it's the kind of question I would ask
if I were writing this poem ten years ago,

    but it isn't—now there's only one good question,
and that's "What the fuck?"
    I mean, your looks do leave, but then
so does everything else: your friends,
       your memories, the people who love you.
    In Galway Kinnell's poem "Parkinson's Disease,"
a man is watching his wife help

    her sick father use the toilet and then lead him
out of the bathroom like a dancer,
    like the girl she was when he was the strong one
and she stood on his shoes and he lifted her as they foxtrotted
       on the living room rug,
    and the man thinks, *she could be teaching him /
the last steps that one day she may teach me,*

    though at the moment the father looks
almost happy, as though *it will be only
    a small dislocation / for him to pass from this paradise
into the next.* And you, you think of the time
       you went back into a restaurant
    to get the hat you'd left, and there's already
another couple at the table where you and your wife were

just a minute before, and you get your hat
and you go back out on the sidewalk,
    and she's there, and she smiles at you,
and you smile back: you're happy now,
        but one of you will leave this world before the other,
    and the one who is left will be so unhappy
that he or she will not want to get up in the morning,

    not be around other people, especially happy ones,
not want to live. After a while, though,
    you will be happy again, and why?
Because you are so happy now.
        E. L. Doctorow says a writer is like a driver at night
    who sees only as far as his headlights will let him,
but who is not? A man rolls ahead confidently

    because he's sure there's a world ahead of him
in the dark even though he can't see it:
    there's a diner with food and hot coffee, and down the road,
a house with a woman who loves him,
        a woman with a bottom as wide as a cello,
    and as he gets closer to that house,
she's lowering herself into a bath. Maybe he'll get home

    while she's still in the tub, and he'll sit on the edge,
and they'll talk, and it'll be sexy,
    but it'll be the sexiness of older people, the kind
where the body of your beloved is not a statue
        you lay across your shoulder and take home
    as a trophy of war, because the wars are over,
they're finished, and the land is green again,

    and you know every hill and valley,
you can see them without looking, feel them and never touch,
    the tips of your fingers like those
of a blind man making his way through

the house he has lived in for years:
   the sun room, the breezeway, the library full of books
he has never opened, the ones he knows by heart.

The movie says that good follows good and bad follows bad. Now, I don't believe that. But I think the world wants to believe that, and that it's best to believe that. If you don't think that way, everything gets a little too complicated.

—John Malkovich on his film *"The Dancer Upstairs"*

All Earthly Hues

> The sweet tinges of sunset skies and woods; yea, and the gilded velvets
> of butterflies, and the butterfly cheeks of young girls. . .
> —Herman Melville

I'm at the funeral of sweet, much-loved old man Ivan Johnson
    in the little antebellum church on Park Avenue,
and Dr. Johnson was so adored that there's no room
        downstairs, so I end up in the "slave gallery,"
and as I look down and wait for the service to begin,

I notice that everyone downstairs has a hymnal,
    but not we children of Paradise. There are no hymnals
upstairs because there are no hymnal *racks* upstairs,
        since slaves weren't literate. So if I had a hymnal,
I'd have to set it down on the rail, and when I got up,

I might knock it off and crack the head
    of some godly planter: "Oh, Lord, I've gone and busted
Squire Carter right in the middle of that big old head
        of his! How I wish he'd have let Miss Lily go on
with those reading lessons—then I'd have had that book

in my hands and not placed it athwart that confounded
    rail and thus occasioned this sad fortuity!"
About this time, the minister, by all outward
        appearances a man of industry, frugality, and sobriety,
begins to shout like a truck-route snake handler!

Alas, the ministry: even the Catholic Church of my youth,
    with its bedizened clergy and Latinate ritual,
has become a shabby, colloquial affair, its sonorities anglicized
        and drawled by a padre dressed more like a camp chaplain
than a duly-anointed representative of His Holiness,

The Pope, himself still multilingual and nattily attired,
    if, for my taste, a bit too unbending on the matter
of birth control. To wit, this reporter has covered this story before,
    and whereas, as a 14 year-old
listening to Father Grifasi at St. Aloysius, I used to plot

military takeovers, calculating how many men I'd need
    and what kind of arms they'd require
to empty the church and send everyone packing,
    now, considerably older and more peaceable,
I find myself thinking, as Pastor Bob natters on,

of three guys with whom I'd had more or less acquaintance
    over the years, first guy being a magician
who was famous for saying that magicians can't play cards,
    because if they win, they look like cheaters,
and if they lose, they look like lousy magicians.

Second guy, named Albert Camous, is a Frenchman
    who was born in Algeria just before World War I
and who moved to France and made a career
    in business, and once, he told me, he was walking
down a Paris street when whom should he run into

but a school chum from his North African days
    who says, "Oh, but Albert, how proud we are,
zuh uzzer boys and I, to 'ave 'ad such a
    distinguished playmate, zuh author of
L'Etranger and *La Chute* and now zuh winner

of zuh *Prix Nobel*," and I could see where this was going,
    I mean, I started to get physically ill
as his story approached an ending as inevitable
    as a car wreck, so to get it over with
as quickly as possible, I put my hand on his arm and said,

"Please don't tell me you told your chum
    you were Albert Camous the businessman
and not Albert Camus the novelist," and Albert Camous
        the businessman looked at me with Gallic
sangfroid and said, "But, of course. Why I would lie to heem?"

He'd broken the heart of his friend and probably missed out
    on an opportunity for a really good free meal,
and all in the name of *la verité*. Third guy's a little kid,
    a pal of mine who called his toothbrush
his "meenter-meinter," and everyone in his family

thought it was so cute they called their toothbrushes
    meenter-meinters, too, and it wasn't until
he went to camp and told one of the other boys that he had
        a really swell-looking meenter-meinter
that he realized what a disservice his adoring parents and siblings

had done him. His name was John Mathis and he's now
    John Mathis the public utility lawyer in California
and not Johnny Mathis the singer,
        whose "Twelfth of Never" is still played
instead of "The Wedding March" by numerous church organists

who can't persuade strong-willed brides otherwise.
        And by the way, folks, that "Wedding March"
was composed by the guy known as Felix Mendelssohn
        to us but as Felix Mendelssohn-Bartholdy
to his mother, Mrs. Bartholdy! My, how the years get away

from one. First time I read Hawthorne, I thought he was anxious
        and unhappy—then I realized I was! 30 years later,
he seems all bold and brave, all full of purpose
        and new ideas, all set to put "the rusty iron frame-work
of society" out by the curb so the Solid Waste Management boys

can heave it on their truck while he and Emerson and Thoreau
    and even Melville, clearly brimming with genius
yet a bit too puppyish in his devotion to a man of whom
        his own wife said, "Hawthorne hates to be touched
more than any other person I know," knock together

their big utopian America of smart, busty women
    and broad-shouldered guys who raise their own vegetables
and churn their own butter and cobble their own shoes
        and free the slaves *and* give Texas back to the Mexicans.
So Hawthorne was right then and he's right now,

and he didn't change a word! Go figure, you epistemologists!
    Oh, *la verité, la verité*—
what in the whole ass-biting *qu'est-ce que c'est*
        is *la verité* in the first place?
According to C. S. Lewis, there weren't enough

dons to grade the lit exams at Oxford during the second
    World War, so one of the faculty
from History was brought in, and he began grading
        quietly enough, but soon he was snorting
with indignation, and after the fifth or sixth exam paper, he said,

"I say, Lewis, your chaps seem to think
    that if something sounds good, it must be true!"
Or you could put it this way: both "We Shall Overcome"
    and "A Change Is Gonna Come"
deal with the same subject, so why is the former

more popular, even though the latter
    is a better song? Probably because "We Shall Overcome"
is easier to memorize; it's repetitive
        and doesn't have any images in it.
Images are the thing, aren't they, reader? Quite the little dealmaker,

those images: when Sam Cooke sings he was born
    by a river in a little tent, you, who were born in
a hospital in Sheboygan or Eau Claire, say,
        "*I* was born by the river! *I,* too, was born in a little tent,"
just as Our Savior was born in a manger in a baking desert,

in a country so dry they didn't even have the word "river"
    in the dictionary! They probably didn't even have dictionaries!
Or if they did, somebody'd say "Look up a word,"
        and somebody else'd say, "Can't! Too hot!"
Winding down from a great I-saw-the-light trumpet blast

about all the sanctified hubba-bubbas waiting upstairs
    for us under God's big sun, Pastor Bob
announces that dapper old man Ivan Johnson is in Heaven
    at this very moment, which I'd say
is a world-class no-brainer, for if there are only two choices,

suffice it to say that Dr. Johnson's not going to end up
    in the Hot Place shoveling brimstone under the supervision
of some sarcastic imp or archfiend. But so it goes in the land
        of the bichromatic, where every act, word, wish, choice,
and aspiration is as white as Squire Carter's big ol' butt cheeks,

as black as the soil of Mother Africa. What about your grays,
    though, your drabs, your duns, not to mention
your Land's End or J. Crew catalog colors, your fawn, taupe, quartz,
        plum, camel? Poor lost Vincent Van Gogh
had this yarn ball made up of odds and ends of different-colored wools

that he would place next to each other until he found
    just the right combination, your red next to your indigo,
your orange between your cerise and your violet but not too close
        to your crimson, your blue, until he said
That's it, that's a world worth living in, that's the one for me.

Mopery With Intent to Creep

on the Ten Commandments

We need them: otherwise life is just a "big-ass cluster fuck,"
    as ex-cop Howard, now my barber,

tells me, referring not to an orgy he'd raided once but a hell-raising,
    a confusion, a righteous old hullabaloo.

Without them, we'd have either what sociologists call the "hidden
    curriculum," i.e., the rules for getting along

in life that everybody knows, even though no one can say
    what they are or how they learned them,

or else a catalog of misdoings as thick as the Manhattan Yellow
    Pages: in the *Aeneid,* the Cumaean Sibyl

tells Virgil she could not name the sins of all the sinners
    in hell if she had "a throat of iron."

With respect to my own compliance, I do well on the first
    two, since I have no god at all

and thus put none before the god of Moses, and I certainly don't
    carve idols. I swear, though. I keep the Sabbath,

if not holy, at least civilized: I do yard work, take long naps,
    listen to music, read to and am read to by

my sweetheart, cook vegetarian or almost. I honored my parents
    when they were alive and do so today

in word, deed, and poem. I have never murdered anyone. I have
    committed very little adultery.

Yes, I have lied and stolen—but I've never murdered anyone
     nor coveted their ox or donkey or male servant.

Therefore my overall score of seven or passing, same as on
     the driver's test. Note that the commandments

don't address such contemporary issues as gay rights, pre-marital
     sex, and physician-assisted suicide.

Note, too, that there are no rewards for good behavior:
     you can get a ticket for running

a red light, but the mayor will not host a reception in your honor
     should you go through a green. Nobody can

get their story straight at Howard's big free-for-all, so when
     he says he's going to arrest everybody

some front-yard Felix Frankfurter sneers, "On what charge?"
     and Howard says, "Mopery with intent to creep!"

Yet as he tells me this, Howard seems wistful more than
     anything else, like the ancient Greek

and Chinese sages who said for the good of the village, we must
     believe in gods who don't exist.

The Measurator

I'm just now meeting Louis Menand, Pulitzer Prize-winning author
    of *The Metaphysical Club,* and I say, "Are your forebears Huguenots,
Mr. Menand?" and he says, "How did you know that?" and I say
    I don't know, and he says no one ever asked him that before,
so how did *I* know, me, and I say I don't know how I know, though later
    I realize it's fairly simple: Mr. Menand's name is classic French,

yet he himself strikes me as very patrician in a New York,
    moneyed-intellectual sort of way, so I'm guessing he didn't just hop
off a boat, therefore his ancestors came over some time before,
    and why would a bunch of Frenchies trade in their yummy cuisine
and fabulous architecture for hot dogs and A-frames
    unless they'd been involuntarily exiled, i.e., were Huguenots?

When I tell this story to my colleague Bob Butler, also
    a Pulitzer Prize-winning author (though for *A Good Scent From
a Strange Mountain,* not *The Metaphysical Club*), Bob says
    that's how psychics work, by picking up little hints they themselves
don't understand and having both the *chutzpah* to go with their hunches
    as well as the BS to back and fill when their hunches turn out to be

totally meshuge. Fair enough, Bob! Indeed, the very next day,
    when I'm talking to grad student Jason Nemec, I say, "Are you
six feet three, Jason?" and he says, "How did you know?"
    But this one's even easier: I'm six feet even, and my son Will Kirby
is six two, meaning I have to look up slightly to make eye contact
    with him, and I have to look just a fraction higher with Jason,

therefore *quod erat pluribus unum ex post facto,* as the old Romans
    had it. That night I see a production of Rossini's little-known opera
Le Comte Ory, in which a man played by a woman pitches woo

to a woman played by a woman who gives another man played by
a man but dressed as a woman the impression that she is pitching
   woo to a woman played by a woman who is really a man

played by—oh, the hell with it. How do we know anything?
   How did ancient peoples know that if you chewed on a willow
twig, you'd get a dose of acetylsalicylic acid, i.e., aspirin? Or that
   the bark of the cinchona tree contained the drug that cured malaria,
i.e., quinine? Who were their scientists and how many double-blind
   studies did they run? For that matter, how does a dyspeptic dog

know to eat one plant in the woods but not a hundred others?
   What kind of scientists do dogs have? I bet the ancient savants
had plenty of involuntary help with their tests: "Y'all sick people
   in this group eat the red plant, and y'all in the other eat the blue,
and the ones that live come and see me in the lodge over yonder
   where I'm having lunch with the chief and them."

In *The Metaphysical Club,* the bottom line is that ideas are
   pretty much zilch, that you do by doing, even if you've never
done before, as in the case of the William James who said
   the first lecture on psychology he heard was the first one he gave
as a psychology professor at Harvard. After the opera, I sleep
   and dream of a universe without ideas, a cosmos dominated

by a wondrous device called The Measurator, a spinning rod
   that measures everything by growing thicker or thinner in
the part given over to the gauging of such-and-such a phenomenon,
   so that if your name were Harold, say, and you wanted to know
how many Harolds were being born at a given moment,
   you'd go stand at that part of the Measurator and watch it

thicken or thin at a faster or slower pace as more or fewer Harolds
   came into or exited the world. And since one kind
of measurement can't pile up on another, the Measurator is horizontal

and extends all the way across the earth and then out into
the sky, so that the only way to find out what's going on
    at one of its distant points is to get into one of the little

bathtub-sized space ships that float to and fro along its axis
    and try not to run into one another as their pilots try
to find out the rate by which the national debt is increasing, say,
    or whether or not there are still any Huguenots.
Myself, I'd like it to measure abstractions, such as
    the disappointment we feel when things don't turn out

as badly as we'd hoped. Maybe it does, way out in the darkness
    of space where we can't see what's happening.
Maybe that's the knowledge God tried to keep from Adam and Eve.
    God the Measurer—though if He is, He's keeping the results
to Himself! Figuring if we don't know how wonderful and
    terrible we are, that's the bad news, yeah, but also the good.

Die Meistersinger

I'm sniffling as I watch *Only the Strong Survive*
　　　and hear Jerry Butler say God called Otis Redding
　　and Sam Cooke, but then I think: If God called
Otis Redding and Sam Cooke, did He also call Hitler
　　and Mussolini? Or did the Devil call Hitler and Mussolini
　　　　and send them to God as a joke? Or did God call Hitler
　　and Mussolini so he could send them to the Devil

and make sure they got to Hell, and if so,
　　　has He sent them already or is He taking His time,
　　and if that's so, why? What if you got to Heaven
and Hitler and Mussolini were there? Once
　　Machiavelli dreamed he saw a band of poorly
　　　　dressed men, so he asked who they were,
　　and they said they were the saintly and blessed

on their way to Heaven, and then he saw a crowd
　　　in noble attire discussing Big Ideas, and among them
　　were Plato, Plutarch, and Tacitus, and again, he asked
who they were, and they said they were the damned.
　　After telling his friends, Machiavelli said he'd be
　　　　happier in Hell chatting excitedly with the all the smart
　　guys than in Heaven, dying of boredom alongside

the saintly. My mother thought Heaven was of
　　　this earth. The crew of the *Bounty*, too: I thought
　　they mutinied against their captain's tyranny,
but turns out it was because they wanted to go back to
　　the Tahiti they'd just left with its warm trade winds,
　　　　fresh fruit, and beautiful, eager women—
　　that instead of freezing on a crowded ship,

being whipped and buggered so they could go home
        to a country where they'd be so poor no one would
    ever love and caress them, to England with its cabbage,
its toothless drabs. Emerson wrote that Napoleon
    was not himself at the Battle of Massena until
        the dead began to fall around him, and then
    "his powers of combination" awoke "and he put on

terror and victory as a robe." Hmm! Very nice
        for Napoleon, I'm sure! Not so nice for the dead,
    though, tumbling before the reaper's scythe
like so many wheat straws in a field, nor for
    the widows and children in the small towns of France,
        gazing worriedly at the horizon and wondering
    "Où est mon mari?" and "Où est mon père?"

Yet I like that phrase "powers of combination."
        We use these when we write poetry or wage war,
    or, for that matter, make a nice meal for our friends—
actually, a really nice meal, because you could make
    a merely nice meal without being that great a cook.
        "Powers of combination" is probably what Emerson
    had in mind when he said "Genius is the activity

which repairs the decays of things." It's what sees
        the glass as half full as opposed to half empty,
    although Emerson didn't say that; that'd be too cornball
an utterance for a big thinker and all-around classy guy
    like Emerson to come up with. Still, I like to read him
        and Nietzsche and Schopenhauer and those kinds
    of guys when I'm perplexed; their advice is just

as good as the crap you get in the self-help books,
        plus their style is a *whole* lot better. Here's
    an Emersonism for you: "Sleep lingers all our lifetime about

our eyes, as night hovers all day in the boughs of the fir-tree." There,
   isn't that better than "Live every day as though it were
      your last"? In the movie, soul Meistersingers like Sam
   Moore tend to echo their future deaths when they say things

   like "I don't want to leave you, but I've got to go."
      Go where? To towel off, probably, and help themselves
   to a big plate of wings and fries. If there is a God,
it's because His powers of combination are better
   than ours. He'd be the best at whatever He chose.
      Best film-maker, best R&B singer, best philosopher,
   best poet, best general—best dictator, even. Best fallen angel.

Hello, I Must Be Going

I'm sitting in a London lecture theater and thinking
of my mother, dead just these three weeks—
    and by the way, ladies and gentlemen, this will not,
repeat, not be one more crappy poem about a dying mother!—
    as I listen to Dr. David Parker speaking on
"Love and Death in Dickens," how the novelist wrote
    about Christmas falteringly in his early work

and then with symphonic fullness when he realized
what was missing, namely, pain, cruelty, death,
    and the bullying of small children, as when everyone
is so mean to Pip, for example, like Mr. Pumblechook,
    who asks the orphan to imagine what it would have
been like if he had been a pig instead of a boy
    and answers for him: "You would have been disposed

of for so many shillings according to the market
price of the article, and Dunstable the butcher
    would have come up to you as you lay in your straw,
and he would have whipped you under his left arm,
    and with his right he would have tucked up
his frock to get a penknife from out of his waistcoat pocket,
    and he would have shed your blood and had your life."

Sheesh! Before *Great Expectations,* says Dr. Parker,
Dickens' attitude to Christmas was close
    to the "fashionable indifference" of John Clare's
Shepherd's Calendar and other similar works,
    but then he took one of his long walks and thought hard
and finally figured out the pain part—showing, not Tiny Tim,
    but Tiny Tim's empty chair—or, better, the way

to use the pain to make readers happy, because,
while it's true that Mr. Pumblechook's meanness
    casts into bright relief the almost saintly sweetness
of Jo Gargery, who answers every threat by covering
    Pip's plate with more and more gravy, that's not
the only way pain works. Because we want the pain.
    We want to cry. We like to feel bad, though not as bad

    as I felt the night I got the call saying Miss Josie only
had a few hours to live. The woman who was with her
    passed the phone to me, and I said, "Hello, Miss Josie!"
and she said, "Hi, David!" and that was the last thing
    anybody heard her say, because within a few minutes
she started to slip away. Billy Collins told me how he sat
    by the bed of his own dying mother, and when he saw that

    her eyes had rolled back but her lips were moving,
the Caribbean lady who sat with her said, "Look, she's traveling."
    So that was the night Miss Josie traveled. Zoom!
Off to the Unknown Country, and without so much as a by-your-leave.
    She was a regular Thane of Cawdor of a woman, my mom;
nothing became her life like the leaving of it. She worked hard,
    she was kind to others, she was grateful for what she had,

    and when it was time for her to go, she didn't grumble;
she just left. And I, who shared her indifference
    to any hope for an afterlife yet feared I might start shouting
for a confessor when my own time comes, I said to myself,
    Yes, that's it, that's what you do. I said to myself,
This is the real knowledge: that there's no knowledge.
    And so, after some initial sniffling and nose-blowing

    and eye-wiping, I found myself not merely reconciled
but so happy I wanted to sing as I walked the streets
    of London, because here I'd been disbelieving
in the afterlife, sure, like most of the overeducated, yet hopeful—

full of hope!—partly because, well, I do want to see
my dead parents again and figure that, after I die, I'll want
      to meet up with my wife and kids for another go-round

      but also because the idea of Paradise is so appealing
in a literary way, much more so than just,
      you know, fucking . . . Buddhistic acceptance, blah blah.
Hence most religions. Hence "Danny Boy"
      and the father singing that when he's in his grave,
he'll hear the son walking above him and then bending low
      to whisper "I love you" so the father can sleep

      until the day the son follows him to wherever.
Hence, too, the eight-year-old girl whose mother
      found her crying because her father had died
in the collapse of the World Trade Center towers
      and she was afraid that when she became
an old woman and died and went to heaven, her father
      wouldn't be able to recognize her.

      But isn't it a little, um, *selfish?* To want someone else
to leave the earth and all its pleasures just so you won't
      be bored down there among the moles and grubworms?
"*La forme, c'est le fond qui remonte à la surface,*"
      says Victor Hugo. Is that what belief is,
the depth which rises to the surface?
      Ah, *la religion, qu'est-ce que c'est,* as wise old Mr. Hugo

      would have it, he who wrote the fabulous Broadway musical
Les Miserables and inspired my friend Roberto G. Fernández
      to begin a novel called *The Miserables,* pronounced,
not *Lay Mizzerob-bluh,* but *Thuh Mizzerabulls.*
      "I no sad!" say many people, "I go to heaven!,"
but I'm not sure they're thinking it through.
      Also, there's one big problem with the afterlife, as I see it,

which is what are you going to say to or do
with all these people that you didn't say or do anything to
    or with when you were up on the surface
going to ball games and cookouts?
    Because if there's only heaven and hell,
they'll be in heaven; you don't go to hell
    for charring the weenies or bobbling an infield fly.

Also, instead of sitting around in the trailer
scratching yourself and mumbling, "We believe our reward's
    in the next world, not this one,"
isn't it just a little more important that you try to do
    good things in the here and now, and by "good things"
I mean not only avoiding the bad behavior of, for example,
    the men in the Italian war camp whom Primo Levi

describes in If This Is a Man who, when they found out
they were going to be sent to Auschwitz, spent the night
    before the train left fighting and fucking each other
but also practicing the good behavior of, for example,
    the women who spent that night making food
and washing the children and cleaning the children's clothes
    for what would be their final journey, so that when

the sun rose the next day, it shone on the tiny shirts
and pants the women had hung on the wire to dry.
    Picasso to Matisse: "When one of us dies,
there will be things that the other will be able
    to say to no one." Okay, but is that so bad?
Oh, sure, you may think you want your departed loved ones
    to reappear the way the dead do in John Marston's

The Malcontent (1604), ridiculous strangers
with big red noses and tufts of hair over their ears
    who pull off their masks and kiss the astonished women
who thought themselves widows and clap pistols

to the heads of those who betrayed them
in the first place. But if I got my mother back,
    she'd still be a sick old lady.

She wouldn't be as I remember her best:
45, still sexy (though I wouldn't have thought so then),
    toiling like a beskirted Hercules at work
and home both, growing champion roses, raising
    horsessheepchickensducksburros,
and cooking every morning and most nights
    for three male ingrates: my father, my brother,

and yours truly, the poet. No, she'd be 99
still and sharp of mind, yet so frail in body
    and weak in sight and hearing that she'd say
"I'm ready to die!" most days of her last year,
    though on others she'd want to know what
the Portuguese are famous for. Or how yogurt is made.
    Or whether popsicles have seeds. Or if the Japanese

have taken over yet. "Not yet!" I'd say, though yogurt
remains a mystery. And it is just one month later that I am in
    Baton Rouge with Barbara and the boys
and my brother and his family, burying my mother's ashes
    and giving away the few things she had left
and taking a few with me as I say goodbye forever
    to the then-little, now medium-sized town I grew up in.

Goodbye, Baton Rouge! Good bye to the City Club,
where my father stayed his first night in 1936.
    Goodbye to the LSU campus, where Dr. Tommy
looked out his classroom window and stopped
    dead in the middle of his Chaucer lecture
when he saw the pretty young chemistry teacher
    and decided he had to meet her, "come what may."

Goodbye to Mike & Tony's and the Italian Garden,
where Doctor Tom used to woo Miss Josie
    over well-done beefsteaks and factory-strength spaghetti sauce.
Goodbye to the tiny grave of Thomas A. Kirby III,
    the brother who should be six years older than I am
but who lived only a day. Goodbye to Moss Side Lane
    and the pond and the barn and the pine patch

    and the three live oak trees, one of which grew
so fast than that my father asked around and found
    it had been planted in what was once a mule cemetery,
years earlier. Goodbye, goodbye to all that!
    And goodbye to all the other little towns
on Interstate 10 that I'd pass on the way over and back!
    Goodbye, Milton, and goodbye, Bagdad,

    that appeared together on a single sign
reading "Milton Bagdad" and always made me think
    of a fat man in a fez and white suit,
like the Sidney Greenstreet character in *Casablanca*.
    And goodbye to Defuniak Springs, the town containing
"fun" in its name but also "aaakk!" or the sound we make
    just before the ax strikes, if we can see it coming.

    Can you imagine what it would be like to live in a country
that doesn't have a town named "Defuniak Springs"?
    No? Good, because you don't have to!
And now that I am back in darling Tallahassee,
    so maligned by so many Frenchmen of my acquaintance
who say to me, "Bot eet moss be so terry-bull to leeve in zis . . .
    zis . . . how do you call heem?—zis Tallahass!",

    neglecting the fact that their own Montaigne
preferred his farm to the huggermugger of Bordeaux,
    I am free to reflect on what a lovely dream it is,
this afterlife. *Pow!* Christ is resurrected, in a burst

of radiance that burns his image into the Shroud of Turin.
Fabulous! And no less fabulous for the fact
　　that spoilsport investigator Joe Nickell wrote a book

in which he described how he used powdered pigments
and a bas-relief statue to create a Shroud of Bing Crosby!
　　Ha, ha! Very funny, Joe! And exceedingly rational to boot.
It's just that you can't stop people from believing
　　in an afterlife or at least hoping that there is one.
In Verona, Dante passed a group of women, one of whom said
　　"Isn't that the man who goes down to Hell as he likes

and returns and brings back news of them below?"
to which another replied, "Indeed, it must be him—
　　do you not see how his beard is singed and his skin darkened
by the heat and smoke that are below?" And Dante is said
　　to have heard the words and passed on, though smiling a little.
Then eight months after Dante's death, his son Jacopo
　　dreamed that his father appeared before him, dressed in white.

Jacopo asked him if he lived, and Dante said, "Yes,
but in the true life, not our life." Oh, isn't that pretty?
　　But isn't "our" a better word than "true"? Our sweetheart.
Our favorite movie. Our mom and dad. Our childhood.
　　Our little town. Our couch, our nap. Our bottle, our glass,
our sandwich. Our dream! That's the deal: it's only a dream.
　　The son with his mother again, the little cripple in his chair.

The Temple Gate Called Beautiful

—Acts 3:2.

It says HELL IS HOT HOT HOT HOT
    and NO SEX WITH MEN ALOUD
and NO ICE WATER IN HELL
    on the hundreds of washers and dryers
        and air conditioner housings that stud
the land around outsider artist W. C. Rice's house in Prattville,
    though Mr. Rice isn't well today,

so I'm chatting through the bedroom window
    of a man I visit every three-four years
to talk a while and then stroll the property
    that offers an ineluctable foreknowledge of The Pit
        to people like me, though Mr. Rice has always been
nice as pie, never proselytizing or even asking
    if I've been saved, which, according to him,

either you are or you aren't. It's like day or night
    with W. C., sun or moon, fish or fowl. Beatles, Stones.
Montague, Capulet. Merchant copy, customer copy. Elvis, Frank:
    there's no Elvis *and* Frank in W. C.'s cosmology,
        no gray area at all, though we all want one, don't we,
we all want to be good, as George Orwell said,
    but not too good, and not all the time, and now

Mr. Rice is telling me about the woman
    who came by at eleven the previous evening
after Mrs. Rice had already tacked up
    the cardboard sign that says it's too late to visit now
        but invites folks to return the next morning,
but the woman was crying so hard, and her teenaged daughter
    and her daughter's friend, too,

that they let her in, and it turned out her husband,
    who'd been physically abusive to her
their whole time together, had himself
    been beaten to death that very afternoon
        by a couple of these Pike County Paladins
who either had a strong sense of how
    the whole karma thing works or, more likely,

    were just repaying him in a familiar currency,
        only more of it, though the event had triggered
in his new widow not a feeling of gladness
    or simply relief but that peculiar remorse
        that overtakes us when somebody dies
that we just hated the shit out of in the first place,
    and now she was asking Mr. Rice if he could say

    where her husband was right now, this very minute,
        like, between this world and heaven, and, if so,
could she pray him up there, and you don't have to have
    a divinity degree from one of the area Bible colleges
        to guess that Mr. Rice's answer was a clear "Nope,"
a definite "He's pretty much where you saw him last,"
    and probably not even the "pretty much"!

    And as Mr. Rice is going on about this concrete
        if somewhat unfeeling application of his belief system,
I'm thinking of how I was reading Andrew Motion's
    new Keats biography last night in room 246
        of the Fairfield Inn in nearby Montgomery
and came across a passage on Sir Astley Cooper,
    Keats' training surgeon at Guy's Hospital,

    the same Sir Astley Cooper who said
        a surgeon must have "an eagle's eye,
a lady's hand, and a lion's heart," and at the time,
    I thought, To what profession do these attributes

not apply? And the answer is,
Mr. Rice's! When some audience members
    booed a drunk Jerry Lee Lewis one time,

he gestured toward the back of the hall
    and said, "Them doors swing both ways."
Not here on Highway 86 near Prattville, though,
    not on Mr. Rice's property. Doors only go one way here;
        you're either safe or out on Mr. Rice's
diamond. You're kosher or treyf. It's Heaven or Hell for you,
    not to put too fine a point on it, and usually Hell.

But as the smart-alecks say, if you go to Hell
    for doing Satan's work up here, why would
he punish you when you got to his place? Some of Mr. Rice's work
    suggests that men in Hell are having sex
        with other men, but if that's what you like. . .
At the Montgomery Museum of Fine Arts
    are paintings by Sargent, Hopper, and Rothko

as well as the sculpture of another outsider artist,
    Charlie "Tin Man" Lucas, who makes animals
out of car parts. Nothing by Mr. Rice in that museum, though:
    the people in charge don't mind if a busload of tourists
        sees a deer made out of shock absorbers,
but they wouldn't want them to pause before a Sargent heiress
    with her silk habiliments and upswept tresses

and Grecian Urn-ish guarantees of immortality
    and then stumble over a rusty Kelvinator
on which someone has painted YOU WILL DIE in red house paint.
    No, the outskirts are right for Mr. Rice,
        not Art's well-appointed townhouse.
You leave Montgomery through the temple gate that leads from town
    to country, and on both sides, look: beautiful.

ENCOUNTER

We were riding through frozen fields in a wagon at dawn.
A red wing rose in the darkness.

And suddenly a hare ran across the road.
One of us pointed to it with his hand.

That was long ago. Today neither of them is alive,
Not the hare, nor the man who made the gesture.

O my love, where are they, where are they going
The flash of a hand, streak of movement, rustle of pebbles.
I ask not out of sorrow, but in wonder.

Wilno, 1936

—Czeslaw Milosz

The Knowledge

I'm outside the Globe in the intermission of *Midsummer*
Night's Dream when whom should I run into but actor Mark Rylance,
   who was so funny as Olivia in *Twelfth Night*
and whose hand I seize because I want to thank him for his remarks
   just before the start of the September 11 performance
      when he came on stage and asked us to remember the horror

of that day and then called for a moment of silence in memory
of the victims, but before I can say anything, he's asking me what I do,
   so I say I'm teaching here in London this fall,
and he asks me what I teach, and I say Shakespeare,
   even though I'm really a poet, and he says, "Ah! A poet!"
      as though he's never met one before, and before I know it,

he knows more about me than I know about him,
and then the little soft bell rings to tell us
   that *Midsummer*'s starting up again
in five minutes, and I still haven't thanked him yet,
   and I'm about to when—typical!—I'm distracted
      by this hat he's wearing, a brown trilby

that's clearly been around a while, and he tells me
that it belonged to the son of his family doctor
   and that the doctor gave it to him
after his, the doctor's, son died,
   and we agree that it's hard to find a good hat these days,
      that it's either a baseball cap that might as well have

a little card with the words "Day Pass" pasted on the crown
or else a Crocodile Dundee type thing
   that's supposed to tell everybody what a turd you are,

and therefore the best hats are the old hats,
    and I tell him I have my dead father's hats,
        and he says he wishes he had his dead father's hats,

        and now the really urgent bell is ringing,
the one that says the play is starting *right now!*
        and I say, "Nice talking to you, Mr. Rylance,"
and he says, "Goodbye now!" and we turn away, but then I turn back,
    because what I want to say is, Ah, Mark, the hats are one thing,
        but don't you really wish you had your *father?*

        The danger in London streets is not from cars
hurtling at you on the "wrong" side
        but from skinny, hyper guys on motorbikes
with big city atlases bungee'd to their windscreens,
    aspiring taxi drivers obtaining what's known in the trade
        as The Knowledge, something they acquire quickly

        by two wheels so they'll know what street is where
by the time they move to four,
        though whenever I take a cab,
there's not a one of them who seems to have the slightest idea
    where I live: "Great Percy Street,"
        I say, and they look at me stone-faced,

        because they're too proud to say they never heard of it,
like I'm, what, making up a name so they can drive around
        looking for a street that doesn't exist
while I call everybody on my "mo-bile"
    and tell them how gullible London cabbies are?
        But then I say, "Yeah, in Islington" or "Near the Angel,"

        and the cabbies almost always get a look on their face
as though they're waking to something
        they knew long ago, in another life, maybe,

a country where they lived once,
  and they had a wife there and kids and lived in a hut
    in a great grassy meadow, and they didn't have any money,

    but you didn't really need money then,
and they never thought of themselves as happy,
    because to think that way, you'd have to know
what unhappiness is, and they didn't know, they just lived there,
    and now it's all coming back, and the cabbie says,
      "Just under Pentonville Road, right? Off Amwell Street?"

    Ah, what would we do if we had The Knowledge?
Wouldn't we be like the beggar who found the ring
    that allowed its possessor to understand
the language of birds, an object so beyond price
    that he couldn't sell it and so died in a mosque courtyard,
      shouting for his mommy, while the mullahs yawned?

    In 1596, Shakespeare's son Hamnet died,
aged eleven, and the playwright's feelings flow
    like cold grey sea water into these lines
from *King John*, which he was writing then:
    "Grief fills up the room of my absent child,
      Lies in his bed, walks up and down with me,

    Puts on his pretty looks, repeats his words,
Remembers me of all his gracious parts,
    Stuffs out his vacant garment with his form,"
and later, "I have heard you say
    That we shall see and know our friends in heaven:
      If that be true, I shall see my boy again."

    And when I read those lines I realize The Knowledge
isn't a sunny globe where everything's marked
    with colored lines—a road here, a river there,

here a mountain, there a town—but a dark planet
   rolling through the indifferent sky,
      silent and empty of love. But then something happens:

      someone calls your name, or they light a cigarette,
or a woman walks by smelling of lilacs,
      of the powder your mother dusted herself with after a bath
when you were a boy and you used to sit on the bed and watch her,
   or a little girl darts into the street after a puppy
      and the oncoming car shrieks to a halt

      and everyone sucks their breath in
and then lets it out slowly, Whewwww,
      and the little girl looks around like, What?
And suddenly a new part of town lights up,
   and as we turn toward it, we notice
      that others are turning also, thousands of them,

      the ones who were left behind the day the planes
exploded into the buildings or that field in Pennsylvania
      and who are now saying "I was ten when my mother died
and I had two brothers, eight and six, and now I'm her age"
   or "What hurt the most was knowing my husband
      and I would never make love again, and now we will,"

      and we can see it in the distance, the part that's lighted now,
and we think we see people there,
      and we try to get closer, but we can't,
and we want to go there, but we don't know what we'll find—
   nothing, maybe, or the torment all over again,
      the pain we thought we'd forgotten but never will.

      Meanwhile, the cabbie's impatient; he shifts
in his seat and he opens the window between you
      and says, "Is that right? Off Amwell Street?"

and you wake as though from another life and look around,
a little dazed, at the lights in the water and the buses
and the throng hurrying over the bridge, and you say, "Sure."

The Secret Room

A poster of two handsome Renaissance gents
catches my eye with the words *Stanze Segrete,* and I think,
Yeah, but whose secret rooms? and then, Who cares,
as long as they're secret? Because almost anyone's
secret room is superior to anyone else's public room.
Even a dog's—*especially* a dog's—secret room,
though not a dog's secrets. When somebody says

secret room to me, I think of the ones you get to
magically: your car breaks down outside an old castle,
and it's pouring, but the butler lets you in, and while
you're drying off in the library and having a brandy
as you wait for the master, you take an old book
off the shelf, but it's the wrong one, or maybe the right,
because just then the wall opens and you find yourself

in a laboratory full of bubbling retorts and cages filled
with the master's sworn enemies, one of whom is now you.
Or the secret rooms that exist in time rather than space—myself,
I'm a pre-Julian calendar man, going for Romulus's
system of ten months that left 61 days uncounted
and unaccounted for on account of the fact that January
and February didn't really exist since there was nothing

for the farmers to do in that part of the year after
the harvest was in and the crops were stored. A good time
was had by all during that period, and what the lord
in his manor and the abbot in his abbey didn't know
didn't hurt them one bit: for two whole months
the entire farm population drank and danced and rogered
one another blind, every haymow and corn crib festooned

with red fannies and spurting dongs and wine jugs
and pretty bosoms shaking like jellies and busted hautboys
and snarled fiddle strings and worn-out wooden clogs
and whatever passed in those days for tiki torches,
crepe paper, Chinese lanterns, angel hair, Christmas crackers,
and those phony cans of candy that have springs inside
that jump out at you like snakes. *O come, O come*

Immanuel: no wonder church and state cracked down
and regulated all the fun out of that Eden, turning it, too,
into a time of alarm clocks, regular church attendance,
hairstyle choices other than the bowl option, bi-annual
dental checkups, induction into the armed forces for those
not nimble enough to avoid it, and eventually, capitalism
in all its tawdry splendor, which, for the purposes of this poem,

includes deceptive ad campaigns, for when I turn up at
the Secret Room show at the Palazzo Medici-Riccardi
and buy my ticket and go in and look around, guess what?
There aren't any! Secret rooms, that is. There's all
the stuff that used to be in the secret rooms, the paintings
and gizmos and statues and hand basins and tapestries
and everything, but the rooms have been remodeled

into non-existence. Talk about secret! There's a door
that used to open into one of the SRs, but it's like any
other door; it could open into a football stadium.
Which presents us with the opportunity to pause here
and ask ourselves just what is a secret room, anyway?
A grave is a secret room: the secret room, I guess.
I wonder what my dad's doing in his grave. Or my mom—

well, not her, because she'd be just a pint or so
of ash and bone, whereas my dad would be some version
of the 5' 11", 172 pound fellow we wept over and kissed
goodbye and lowered into the earth one gray February

morning. What was he thinking before he went there?
80 years old and carving the *Pietà* for his own tomb, Michelangelo
drops his lantern one night and cries, *I am so old that Death*

    often pulls me by the cloak to make me go with him,
   and my body one day will fall like this lantern, and the light
of life will go out, just as that light dies in the young as well:
    a colleague tells me that a student disappeared from
  my university's international study program in this very city,
and when I say, "When did he come back?" she says, "He didn't—
    he disappeared" and I say, "Yeah, I know, but for how long"

    and she says, "For forever, he's gone, he didn't come back,
  he never will," even though his father came to Florence to look
for him, and the police dragged the river, and the dad went
    home and came back again, certain by now that his boy
  wasn't wandering around in a state of amnesia or in a cage
somewhere but was dead, was buried up in the hills, maybe,
    if he was buried at all, and so the father comes and goes

    in his own head, the most secret room of all. One night
  after dinner I tell Barbara I just want to clear my mind
and walk out for fifteen minutes or so and then back again,
    but I end up going all the way down Borgo La Croce
  and across Piazza Beccaria, past the last trattoria and masonry,
past a monumental church, that of San Giovanni Bosco,
    the patron saint of chocolate milk, past the alley

    where the last junkies cackle or drift into unquiet sleep,
  past the garbage a dog paws through and the last graffiti,
all the way to the open window where the last family is having
    dinner together, the children happy yet polite, the mother
  as warm as a flame, and only the father a little thoughtful,
I'm thinking as I stand just outside the light, as though
    he knows something, though even he isn't sure what it is.

Letter Home on My Birthday, November 29, 2002

> A painting in a museum probably hears more foolish remarks than
> anything else in the world.
>
> —Edmond and Jules de Goncourt

Well, that painting never rode with me on a London bus!
    What rubbish the English spout, especially when
they're shouting into what they call their "mo-biles."
    "Hullo," says the woman in front of me, "hullo, hullo!
    I say, don't shout! Hullo?" And then one chap wishes another

an 'appy Thanksgiving, and at first I think, Thanksgiving?
    and then sure, why not, we already sold them Hallowe'en,
and we *did* rid them of a bunch of pesky Puritans,
    so why not turkey, cranberry sauce, and sweet potatoes,
        with or without the little burned marshmallows on top?

Or maybe I just heard wrong: every schoolchild thinks
    that the dying Lord Nelson said "Kiss me, Hardy"
as he lay mortally wounded on the quarter deck of HMS *Victory*,
    whereas what he really said was "Kismet, Hardy,"
        as in Fate, Destiny, All She Wrote, The Big Casino,

Our Records Show Your Policy Has Lapsed, Mr. Nelson.
    Or maybe I heard right but didn't understand:
the night before, we see the whirling dervishes at the Royal Albert Hall,
white-skirted mystics spinning in praise of Allah,
    but even though the MC says it's a religious ceremony

and we shouldn't applaud, we good liberal Westerners can't help
    but show our resounding approval of the Sufi masters,
which means half the audience cheers as lustily as though

the local lads are winning the test match as the other half
    tries vainly to silence them. So many . . . *phenomena!*

So little wisdom. After Thanksgiving, the second big celebration
    in November is founded on the historical truth that,
in a little manger outside Baton Rouge, Louisiana, a child was born
    who happens to be your present hero. So today we are felicitating
        this avatar of all things fungible, not to say nugatory,

    in the human spirit by going to Bates' Gentlemen's Hatters
        Since 1783 in Jermyn Street to buy him a stylish lid.
It's a narrow store: nothing but hats, floor to ceiling, and not those
    look-at-me-'cause-I'm-a-fucking-idiot-type affairs,
        either, but real hats, stylish numbers your Cary Grant

or your Gary Cooper would be tickled pink in.
    Out of the darkness scuttles this diminutive being who instantly
figures me for a "soize fifty-noine," and within minutes
    I emerge sporting a gray felt trilby, wondering if the gnome
        were Bates himself, not only undiminished by 219 years

    of indoor living but unerring in his assessment of cranial diameters.
        But then we go to the British Museum to see
the Piranesi prints; on our way out , the guy behind me vuh-vuh-vuh—
    BLOOOORCH!—he vomits all over me! Barbara drags me
        into the Baby Changing Room to towel me off as best she can,

    and I'm telling you, reader, even the babies don't like it very much!
        They throw their fat legs in the air and howl, not that they smell
all that great to me. Also, I'm sure you'll believe me when I say
    I have my choice of any seat I want on the #19 bus back to Islington!
        So you now know it's not all gray felt trilbies over here.

    That night we dine at Lindsay House in Romilly Street,
        and when I order the grouse, the maître d' leans over and tells me
solemnly he's afraid they are "shot grouse, sir" and for a moment

I don't take his meaning, but when I do, I beam at him speechlessly
and then blurt, "You are, like, so excellent!" and, sure enough,

soon find myself spitting out the little lead pellets with a *buh-ding!*
and thinking how brutal that the grouse are slain at the apogee
of their flight from earth, poor dears, but then, just as quickly,
how happy it is that they are not only blind to the barrel
that's pointed their way but deaf as well to the annihilating bang,

and also how less than fortunate are so many of we the human,
subject as we are to every variety of disorder both infectious
and degenerative, with no guarantees that our *medicos* will be
any more skilled than 19th century frontier surgeon Robert Liston,
soi-disant fastest saw in the west, his record being the procedure

during which he amputated the leg of his patient (who died
of gangrene), sliced off the fingers of his assistant (who also
died of gangrene), and severed the coattails of a spectator
(who died from fright on the spot), thus completing in under
two and half minutes the only operation in medical history

with a mortality rate of 300 per cent! Oh, well, say the theists,
it's not so bad, this way you get to see The Redeemer
that much sooner, no waiting, no siree. Yeah, that'd be okay
if God turned out to be as benign as He is in the story books,
but what about what Heine said? Heine said, "There is a God,

and his name is Aristophanes." What if God were a lot more
interested in playwrighting than in making sure we had
a big fat cushion to sit on throughout Eternity? *Buh-ding!*
How fortunate are the birds of the air not to be caged in a pen
but to soar into the dying sun, the only way to go.

Mountain With Dead People and Dogs

Monte Ceceri, near Florence, where Leonardo's glider was launched in 1505

Flapping my arms for warmth, I start to make my way
down Leonardo's mountain, then realize I don't have
to return the way I came, that there's another path leading—well,
I don't know, exactly, though the trail is clearly marked,
so I take the new path instead, and as I make my way,

in my head I'm translating as best I can the poem of his
that's on the monument at the peak: *The great bird / will
lift in first flight,* it says, *from the top / of mighty
Cecero, / filling the universe / with wonder, / filling all
the histories / with its fame.* Or not: as Girolamo Cardono

said of Leonardo in 1550, "He tried to fly but in vain.
However, he was an excellent painter." At the foot
of the mountain, I was cold but grew hot as I climbed,
though now it's windy and I'm cold again and also
a little unsettled because I'm starting to get that feeling I've had

lately when I think I'm going to see my dead parents
again, a sensation somewhere between fear and hope and one
I get only when I'm alone, because when I'm walking
with Barbara, it never happens, though when I'm by
myself, sometimes I think I'm going to see them, back from

the underworld and—what? Reproaching me, weeping,
saying they're unhappy there, they wish they were
on earth again, or laughing, saying how much they loved me,
how the next life is the true life, not like this
one at all, and would they be naked, would they be shivering

as I am now, would they be wearing what they used
to wear back in Baton Rouge, would they be dressed
like Italians or space aliens in unisex jump suits
        or the ancients in the woodcuts that illustrate
The Inferno and *The Aeneid,* all togas and crowns of laurel?

        By now the sun is nearly down and the wind has begun
to sigh a little in the cedar branches as I realize I'm not alone
on the path: I hear a voice below me and see movement through
        the trees, and even though this is not an especially
scary part of the world except in the sense that one is always

        a little apprehensive about meeting strangers
(how many? are they armed? drunk?) when one is far
from shops and people and police cars, in the Middle Ages,
        real brigands lived in run-down castles in these hills,
men with names like Guido Guerra and Guido Bevisangue,

        warlords who killed other people the way you and I
might sneeze. Which one would you rather run into in
the course of your mountain sojourn, reader? "Guido Blood Drinker"
        is more colorful, but there's something primal
about "Guido War" that makes my blood run even colder

        and that I try to throw off by imagining what it's like
to actually have such a name: "Can I make a reservation?"
"Well, I don't know. How many, and when do you want
        to come in?" "Party of two, eight p.m. Name's War."
"Ah—Mr. War! Yes, sir, Mr. War, anything you say, sir!"

        If your name was Doménikos Theotokópoulos
and you called the same restaurant and the guy asked you
what your name was and you said "Doménikos
        Theotokópoulos," I bet he'd say, "Right—party
of two, eight p.m., name's El Greco," and that'd be that.

What names are we given in the other life?
For that matter, what name is the other life given?
As it turns out, there's nothing to worry about,
    or less than nothing, actually: to my relief (because
I'm happy not to be murdered) and then dismay

    (because I was feeling pretty macho up to this point),
I meet a sixtyish woman with an upswept hairdo wearing
makeup, jewelry, and at least a couple of thousand dollars'
    worth of designer pants and jacket. What's she doing
here? Even worse, she has with her one of those dogs

    that looks like the love child of a mosquito and a carpet
brush, the kind that can only walk ten paces or so
before it has to be picked up and carried, and this one
    is, in fact, limping and looking miserable and clearly
signaling that it's time for a ride, though when I give

    the lady a *Buona sera!* that she returns cautiously,
because even though I am a candy-ass in my own eyes,
I suppose I look capable of mischief to someone like her,
    the dog comes to life and begins to sniff and circle
and wriggle as though in search of something he can't find,

    much like the contraband-sniffing beagles you see
around luggage carousels in your major airports.
Then again, there's so much I don't understand:
    the night before, I am lying in bed and contemplating
whether or nor I really want to take such a strenuous

    hike as I am now taking, when suddenly a scream
barrels across the courtyard like a burning owl: it's either
"Darling, remind me in the morning, and I'll stop by
    the bakery after work and get you one of those
raisin buns you like" or "So! Here you are at last,

your pockets empty, having spent everything on
your friends, the gamblers—*and* the whores!" I'm betting on
the latter. But since she's screaming in Italian, I'll never know,
    for try as I may, my Italian's stuck permanently
    in second gear, and nothing I do can goose it up into third,

    as when I'm buying bread in the bread store
or trying to get my dry cleaning back from the dry cleaner's
and say *Buon giorno* or *Come va?* and the guy behind the counter
    looks up and smiles and lets rip an artillery burst
    of idiomatic Italian and I just grab my shit and keep moving,

    just as I keep moving down the side of this mountain,
and ten minutes later I meet another walker with
yet another dog. I'm glad I didn't meet him first: this one is
    a murderous-looking fellow, wild-haired and stocky,
    though this time he's the one who offers the cordial greeting.

    He has a dog to match, a big bear cub of a mutt,
    though this one, too, begins to sniff and scratch
like the devils in the frescoes by Luca Signorelli in the Duomo
    at Orvieto that show tons of green- and red-rumped
    and blue-winged demons biting and tearing the flesh

    of the wicked dead, whipping and leashing them
    like dogs and shoving and tossing them all around Hell's floor
while, on the other side of the arch, the good dead are pulling
    themselves out of the earth, which is not hard for them
    to do since they're all so broad-shouldered and robust,

    each fellow sporting a great juicy sausage that bounces
    along merrily on a bulging pouchful of nuts,
each chubby-bosomed maid confected of downy peach clefts,
    of blood oranges as drippy and sweet as the ones
    sold by the *fruttivendolo* crying his wares in the piazza!

Indeed, the good dead look so yummy that at first
    I'm jealous, thinking I haven't looked like that in thirty years,
if ever, and then angry, because I don't see my parents here,
        don't see Dr. Tommy and Miss Josie in
        the frail beauty of their old age, which is when I remember

    my scripture and say, Hey, wait a minute,
    I am looking at them and at myself as I'll be after they
and I wake from our sleep beneath the forgetful earth
        clothed in the flesh that was once ours,
        even a muscular, sexy bravado we never had in the first place.

    By the time I encounter my third dog and human
    on the trail down the mountain and witness the same puzzling
canine behavior, I can't help saying, *Che succede con il cane?*
        to the elderly gentleman with the newspaper
        under his arm as his terrier runs circles around me, yipping

    in bewilderment, and in the way educated Europeans
    always do, the man sizes me up as someone whose Italian
is vastly inferior to his English and barks: "HE WANT TO KNOW
        WHERE IS YOUR DOG!" "Uh, *scusi?*" I say.
    "ALWAYS WHEN HE MEET SOMEONE HE HAVE A DOG

    SO HE IS LOOKING FOR YOUR DOG!" "Oh, well,"
    I say, "I don't have no dog," feeling somewhat embarrassed,
as though I've shown up at a black-tie affair in my gym clothes,
        which is about when I remember the story
        of the little boy who couldn't figure out whether Santa Lucia

    brought him his presents at Christmas or whether it was
    his parents, so his teacher tells him that if he believes
in Santa Lucia, then what he wishes for will happen, and
        if he doesn't, it'll be okay, that his parents will give him
        presents anyway, and I think too of how Benvenuto Cellini

wrote that he believed in God, as when his enemy
Luigi Pulci was making his horse prance before a pretty
courtesan and fell, landing with such force that "his right leg
    was broken short off" and he died, prompting the sculptor
    to say *even so may it be seen that God keeps account*

    of the good and the bad, and gives to each one
what he merits, yet when he goes to the Coliseum
with the priest-turned-necromancer who tells him that,
    to fill the old ruin with devils, he must have with him
    a child "of the purest virginity," the little fellow he brings

    from his workshop begins to cry that *a million*
of the fiercest men are swarming around and threatening us,
so Cellini tells the boy, *What you see is only smoke and shadow;*
    so then raise your eyes. Maybe that's it, I think as I raise
    my own eyes to greet the moon—maybe the pope is infallible,

    though not always, and maybe contraception
is murder, yet only for those who feel that way.
Maybe only babies think they have to choose between God
    and the devil, and maybe you should believe in the one
    but not the other, even though you, too, are afraid.

    But what names do we give to good, to evil?
In Signorelli's fresco, the Anti-Christ looks like Jesus,
but what did Jesus look like, and what did his friends call him?
    Did they call him "buddy" or "pal" or "Son of Man"
    or just "man," as in "Hey, man, let's go to Cana" or "Man,

    we better go—those centurions are, like, pissed."
And you, reader: what name do you give yourself?
Say we are two dogs, I the smaller nervous one, and you
    the big good dog who scares everyone when they first
    see it, but then you put your face in their hands as though

saying, "I'm so happy—my master's a nice fellow,
    but you're the one, really, you are," only we're playing now,
you and I, we're jumping on each other, and I put my mouth
        around your leg and shake it, but I don't really bite,
    and you give me a shove with your forepaws and I roll over

        and over in the dirt. And then something happens
    to me. Or to you—you could call it death, you could call it
a thousand things—and suddenly a great bird lifts from
        the top of the rock where we stand. Are you not
    that bird? And I am the little dog still, looking up in wonder.

Sex and Candy

Candy: it's the nookie of children. For when you are a child,
        candy is what you think about during
every waking moment. It's something you can't get from yourself
        and for which, therefore, you depend on the kindness of others.
It's what you hide from other children when you do get some,

what you devour greedily when you have it and bitterly lament
        the absence of when you don't, what's bad for you if you have
too much of it, and so on. Whereas, when you are grown, while candy
        retains some allure, now it is sex that you think about
all the time, what you hide from other adults when you get it, and so on.

So would a divinity student say either candy or sex is a belief system?
        Maybe they're practices, like Buddhism or Quakerism,
rather than belief systems like Roman Catholicism or football.
        Certainly sex was a practice to this fellow I used to know
in college who had all these elaborate schemes for getting women

and who actually succeeded at them, not because the schemes
        were any good—for the most part, they were pretty dumb,
as a matter of fact, as when he got excited when he saw that one
        of the objects of his desire wore a wedding ring
"because that means they do it" or when one smoked,

a sure sign of a moral flexibility—but because the schemes
        were a bridge between his desires and their fulfillment,
a way to get from point A to point B, as it were,
        just as he must have had similarly-successful schemes
for wheedling candy out of his parents when he was young.

Of course, sex is a slightly more complex field of study,
          as I realized when I asked a nonagenarian German gentleman
of my acquaintance what single thing he'd like to have now
     from his student days, when he spent his mornings reading Goethe
and Schiller and his afternoons dueling with sabers

and his nights emptying stein after stein of lager, and the old gentleman,
          who'd been retired for more years than he'd worked
and who still had the scars from saber cuts on his cheeks, smiled
     and pointed toward his belt and leaned close and whispered,
"*Ein Steifer!*" and you don't have to have a Ph. D. in German

to know that's one of those words that must mean pretty much
          what it sounds like! But while he was talking about sex,
I also think he was being not only funny but also nostalgic
     for his dead wife, just as we are all sentimental about those
whom we love, yet when we look around, where are they?

Perhaps they are eating candy in heaven, just shoveling it in.
          Now let's say they're waiting for us
because they want to have sex with us—heavenly sex!—
     though in the meantime, they get to have all the candy they want.
But when we get there, they won't want either one, and neither will we,

and instead, we'll all want the thing that's better than either sex
          or candy, the thing that we got just a glimmer of once,
like a firefly in a distant meadow that we saw one night
     as we were stuffing our faces or pulling somebody's pants down,
and it's got a name, that thing, we just don't know what it is.

The Mysteries

My new friend Mario Materassi has invited me to dinner
at his apartment in Piazza Indipendenza but has cautioned
     me to make sure I ring his doorbell, not that of the other
Materassi, whom Mario describes as *a sworn enemy,*
     but since I've lost the piece of paper with the directions on it,

I don't know whether the button for the Materassi I want
is the one at the top or the one just below it. If I get
     the right Materassi, I'll have a nice dinner and, no doubt,
some of the finest wines known to humanity, whereas
     the wrong one might lunge at me, crying "*Turco! Turco!*"

or "Turk! Turk!" as did the Gonzaga family
of Renaissance Mantua, who derided *their* sworn enemy
     even as they took unto themselves his murderous mojo,
much as we did with the Native American tribes
     whom we cheated and slaughtered and then made into

mascots for our sports teams. So which button?
There's a mystery at hand, terrible yet enticing:
     no wonder the medieval guilds guarded jealously
the *mysteries* of their professions and even called
     themselves *mysteries,* which is not so mysterious

when you consider that, yes, *mystery* derives from Classical
Latin *mysterium* or *mystery* but is also related to
     Medieval Latin *misterium* or job, which word is more
clearly reflected in the Italian *mestiere* (or job),
     one known even to us monolinguists from French *métier*

(or job) which has been transformed into English metier (job).
In those days, painters belonged to the guild
        of the *Speziali* or Pharmacists because they used
arcane formulas in the making of their pigments,
        and there were other secrets as well: Vasari wrote

        that Andrea del Castagno murdered Domenico Veneziano,
from whom he learned the esoteric art of oil painting,
        out of envy, but he can't have, since Domenico outlived
Andrea by four years; still, everybody liked the story:
        Andrea came from a remote village in the mountains

        and there is a wildness in his art that suggests a love
of crime. Artists like Paolo Uccello and Piero della Francesca
        gave up everything to study perspective,
though there was nothing new about it: Pliny the Elder
        claimed that the method of representation

        known as *imagines obliquae* or "slanting images"
was invented in the sixth century B.C. by Kimon
        of Kleonai, yet Plato had condemned perspective
as a "deceit," and the technique was abandoned
        in the Middle Ages in favor of "true" proportions.

        Ah, Paolo, Donatello said, *this perspective
of yours is making you abandon the certain for the uncertain,*
        and Paolo wasn't the only one: in politics, experiments
in government lead to a breakdown in social order; in painting,
        a flat surface can be made to seem round, just as the earth,

        which appears flat, is said by the scientists to be round, after all.
In other words, Perspective can mean *scientific control of
        physical space* or simply *that's how I see it, goddamn it,*
see the whole megillah as tragedy, comedy, history, pastoral,
        pastoral-comical, historical-pastoral, tragical-historical,

tragical-comical-historical-pastoral, scene individable, or poem
unlimited, as the man says. In other words, there is more
        than a single perspective to the word perspective! Ha, ha!
For example, who are the three men in contemporary dress
    in the foreground of Piero's *Whipping of Christ* who talk

    among themselves, indifferent to their Savior's suffering?
And who, I asked myself the other day, are those boys
        I see a hundred yards away? I could tell they were on
their outing, these boys, because of the way they band together,
        not laughing and stopping at shop windows like American students

    or beer drinkers from Germany and Austria
but stumbling elbow to elbow like clumsy soldiers, free for the day
        from their hospital or whatever it's called,
yet it isn't until they're almost on me that I realize they're my age,
        they're in their fifties and sixties, yet they hold hands

    the way children do, have the same childlike haircuts,
same pants pulled too high, same shirts with every button
        buttoned, right up to the neck. I want to say, Boys,
I'm an orphan, too! and think how often, in the midst
    of unbearable sadness, there are moments of strange beauty:

    a father doesn't know that terrorists from Chechnya
have already taken over the building as he walks his children
        to their first day of school in Ossetsia, noting the balloons
the children have, the flowers and presents they're bringing
    to their teachers, and then he walks to his flat 100 meters

    away, and when he hears the pop-pop-pop of gunfire,
he runs to the balcony, where he sees hundreds of balloons
        floating skyward: the frightened children have let go of them
at the same time. Or, after the mafia killed them with
    a bomb under the road leading from the airport to Palermo,

the funeral for Judge Falcone and his wife and three
of their escort at which the 23-year-old widow of one
   of the bodyguards, a Rosaria Schifani, little more than
a girl herself, sobbing for her lost husband as she stands
   to address the audience, saying *My Vito Schifani, he was*

so beautiful and *he had such beautiful legs* and then crying
out in anger, telling the politicians and officials who crowd
   the church that they are as guilty as the man who pressed
the detonator: *I pardon you but get down on your knees*
   and then, in a torrent of fragments, *too much blood*

and *there's no love here, there's no love here, there's no*
love here, there's no love at all. Where is love? What is
   the knowledge? Is it that there is no knowledge or is it
something more? Standing before the doorbell of Mario
   and the other Materassi, I put my finger on the top button

and then the bottom one and then the top one again,
and I turn and look out at the square, where the night
   has come early, with the cold winds that blow down
from the Apennines, and a mother shoos her children
   home, a girl and her younger brother, and a couple passes,

like the lovers in Lampedusa's *The Leopard,* perhaps,
these being *the best years in their lives, but they didn't know it*
   and pursued a future they reckoned more substantial,
though it turned out to be made of smoke
   and wind. And the last old man folds his newspaper but sits

on the bench just a minute more, as cold as it is,
as though he can't bear to leave, and then he, too, goes.
   And without looking back, I reach behind me and push
the first button I touch, and somewhere
   in the building there are feet on the stairs, and a door opens.

To prepare for a book that is concerned to a great extent with the underworld, I read various editions of *The Epic of Gilgamesh, The Iliad, The Inferno, The Odyssey, The Aeneid,* and *The Vision of Tundal,* a twelfth-century account of an Irish knight's trip through Hell. Where possible, I consulted several translations, because I found that a phrase which caught my eye in one version might be rendered in a more engaging way in another. I also watched *Bubba Ho-Tep,* the documentary about Elvis and JFK battling an ancient Egyptian mummy for the souls of the rest of us.

Of the eighteen poems included here, five in particular trudge along in the stygian path of these source materials: "Elvis, Be My Psychopomp," "Merry Hell," "Doughboy's Bitch," "Dogs Who Are Poets and Movie Stars," and "Mopery With Intent to Creep." In these poems, the sources I mention are alluded to, paraphrased, and sometimes briefly quoted.

Door to a Noisy Room, Peter Waldor
Beloved Idea, Ann Killough
The World in Place of Itself, Bill Rasmovicz
Equivocal, Julie Carr
A Thief of Strings, Donald Revell
Take What You Want, Henrietta Goodman
The Glass Age, Cole Swensen
The Case Against Happiness, Jean-Paul Pecqueur
Ruin, Cynthia Cruz
Forth A Raven, Christina Davis
The Pitch, Tom Thompson
Landscapes I & II, Lesle Lewis
Here, Bullet, Brian Turner
The Far Mosque, Kazim Ali
Gloryland, Anne Marie Macari
Polar, Dobby Gibson
Pennyweight Windows: New & Selected Poems, Donald Revell
Matadora, Sarah Gambito
In the Ghost-House Acquainted, Kevin Goodan
The Devotion Field, Claudia Keelan
Into Perfect Spheres Such Holes Are Pierced, Catherine Barnett
Goest, Cole Swensen
Night of a Thousand Blossoms, Frank X. Gaspar
Mister Goodbye Easter Island, Jon Woodward
The Devil's Garden, Adrian Matejka
The Wind, Master Cherry, the Wind, Larissa Szporluk
North True South Bright, Dan Beachy-Quick
My Mojave, Donald Revell
Granted, Mary Szybist
The Captain Lands in Paradise, Sarah Manguso
Pity the Bathtub Its Forced Embrace of the Human Form, Matthea Harvey
The Arrival of the Future, B.H. Fairchild
The Art of the Lathe, B.H. Fairchild

ALICE JAMES BOOKS has been publishing exclusively poetry since 1973. One of the few presses in the country that is run collectively, the cooperative selects manuscripts for publication through both regional and national annual competitions. New regional authors become active members of the cooperative, participating in the editorial decisions of the press. The press, which historically has placed an emphasis on publishing women poets, was named for Alice James, sister of William and Henry, whose fine journal and gift for writing went unrecognized within her lifetime.

Typeset and Designed by Mike Burton

Printed by Thomson-Shore
on 50% postconsumer recycled paper
processed chlorine-free